CASH
BREAKDOWN
forms by showversation
AF812104

Stay *focused*

"It's not how much money you make, but how much money you keep, how hard it works for you, and how many generations you keep it for."

Cash Breakdown

Date:

CASH ENVELOPES/SINKING FUNDS

CATEGORY	AMOUNT	BANKING WITHDRAWAL DENOMINATIONS					
		$1	$5	$10	$20	$50	$100
		Total Number of Each Bill					
TOTAL	$						

INCOME

INCOME SOURCE	AMOUNT	Salary/Wages	Investment	Business	Side-Hustle
Rollover from previous week		☐	☐	☐	☐
		☐	☐	☐	☐
		☐	☐	☐	☐
		☐	☐	☐	☐
		☐	☐	☐	☐
		☐	☐	☐	☐
		☐	☐	☐	☐
		☐	☐	☐	☐
		☐	☐	☐	☐
Total Income	$				
minus - Total Cash Envelopes	$				
Remaining Balance	$				

Double Check It! Calculations

Cash Breakdown

Date:

CASH ENVELOPES/SINKING FUNDS

CATEGORY	AMOUNT	BANKING WITHDRAWAL DENOMINATIONS					
		$1	$5	$10	$20	$50	$100
		Total Number of Each Bill					
TOTAL	$						

INCOME

INCOME SOURCE	AMOUNT	Salary/Wages	Investment	Business	Side-Hustle
Rollover from previous week		☐	☐	☐	☐
		☐	☐	☐	☐
		☐	☐	☐	☐
		☐	☐	☐	☐
		☐	☐	☐	☐
		☐	☐	☐	☐
		☐	☐	☐	☐
		☐	☐	☐	☐
		☐	☐	☐	☐
Total Income	$				
minus - Total Cash Envelopes	$				
Remaining Balance	$				

Double Check It! Calculations

Cash Breakdown

Date:

CASH ENVELOPES/SINKING FUNDS

CATEGORY	AMOUNT	BANKING WITHDRAWAL DENOMINATIONS					
		$1	$5	$10	$20	$50	$100
		Total Number of Each Bill					
TOTAL	$						

INCOME

INCOME SOURCE	AMOUNT	Salary/Wages	Investment	Business	Side-Hustle
Rollover from previous week		☐	☐	☐	☐
		☐	☐	☐	☐
		☐	☐	☐	☐
		☐	☐	☐	☐
		☐	☐	☐	☐
		☐	☐	☐	☐
		☐	☐	☐	☐
		☐	☐	☐	☐
		☐	☐	☐	☐
Total Income	$				
minus - Total Cash Envelopes	$				
Remaining Balance	$				

Double Check It! Calculations

Cash Breakdown

Date:

CASH ENVELOPES/SINKING FUNDS

CATEGORY	AMOUNT	BANKING WITHDRAWAL DENOMINATIONS					
		$1	$5	$10	$20	$50	$100
		Total Number of Each Bill					
TOTAL	$						

INCOME

INCOME SOURCE	AMOUNT	Salary/Wages	Investment	Business	Side-Hustle
Rollover from previous week		☐	☐	☐	☐
		☐	☐	☐	☐
		☐	☐	☐	☐
		☐	☐	☐	☐
		☐	☐	☐	☐
		☐	☐	☐	☐
		☐	☐	☐	☐
		☐	☐	☐	☐
		☐	☐	☐	☐
Total Income	$				
minus - Total Cash Envelopes	$				
Remaining Balance	$				

Double Check It! Calculations

Cash Breakdown

Date:

CASH ENVELOPES/SINKING FUNDS

CATEGORY	AMOUNT	BANKING WITHDRAWAL DENOMINATIONS					
		$1	$5	$10	$20	$50	$100
		Total Number of Each Bill					
TOTAL	$						

INCOME

INCOME SOURCE	AMOUNT	Salary/Wages	Investment	Business	Side-Hustle
Rollover from previous week		☐	☐	☐	☐
		☐	☐	☐	☐
		☐	☐	☐	☐
		☐	☐	☐	☐
		☐	☐	☐	☐
		☐	☐	☐	☐
		☐	☐	☐	☐
		☐	☐	☐	☐
		☐	☐	☐	☐
Total Income	$				
minus - Total Cash Envelopes	$				
Remaining Balance	$				

Double Check It! Calculations

Cash Breakdown

Date:

CASH ENVELOPES/SINKING FUNDS

CATEGORY	AMOUNT	BANKING WITHDRAWAL DENOMINATIONS					
		$1	$5	$10	$20	$50	$100
		Total Number of Each Bill					
TOTAL	$						

INCOME

INCOME SOURCE	AMOUNT	Salary/Wages	Investment	Business	Side-Hustle
Rollover from previous week		☐	☐	☐	☐
		☐	☐	☐	☐
		☐	☐	☐	☐
		☐	☐	☐	☐
		☐	☐	☐	☐
		☐	☐	☐	☐
		☐	☐	☐	☐
		☐	☐	☐	☐
		☐	☐	☐	☐
Total Income	$				
minus - Total Cash Envelopes	$				
Remaining Balance	$				

Double Check It! Calculations

Cash Breakdown

Date:

CASH ENVELOPES/SINKING FUNDS

CATEGORY	AMOUNT	BANKING WITHDRAWAL DENOMINATIONS					
		$1	$5	$10	$20	$50	$100
		Total Number of Each Bill					
TOTAL	$						

INCOME

INCOME SOURCE	AMOUNT	Salary/Wages	Investment	Business	Side-Hustle
Rollover from previous week		☐	☐	☐	☐
		☐	☐	☐	☐
		☐	☐	☐	☐
		☐	☐	☐	☐
		☐	☐	☐	☐
		☐	☐	☐	☐
		☐	☐	☐	☐
		☐	☐	☐	☐
		☐	☐	☐	☐
Total Income	$				
minus - Total Cash Envelopes	$				
Remaining Balance	$				

Double Check It! Calculations

Cash Breakdown

Date:

CASH ENVELOPES/SINKING FUNDS

CATEGORY	AMOUNT	BANKING WITHDRAWAL DENOMINATIONS					
		$1	$5	$10	$20	$50	$100
		Total Number of Each Bill					
TOTAL	$						

INCOME

INCOME SOURCE	AMOUNT	Salary/Wages	Investment	Business	Side-Hustle
Rollover from previous week		☐	☐	☐	☐
		☐	☐	☐	☐
		☐	☐	☐	☐
		☐	☐	☐	☐
		☐	☐	☐	☐
		☐	☐	☐	☐
		☐	☐	☐	☐
		☐	☐	☐	☐
		☐	☐	☐	☐
Total Income	$				
minus - Total Cash Envelopes	$				
Remaining Balance	$				

Double Check It! Calculations

Cash Breakdown

Date:

CASH ENVELOPES/SINKING FUNDS

CATEGORY	AMOUNT	BANKING WITHDRAWAL DENOMINATIONS					
		$1	$5	$10	$20	$50	$100
		Total Number of Each Bill					
TOTAL	$						

INCOME

INCOME SOURCE	AMOUNT	Salary/Wages	Investment	Business	Side-Hustle
Rollover from previous week		☐	☐	☐	☐
		☐	☐	☐	☐
		☐	☐	☐	☐
		☐	☐	☐	☐
		☐	☐	☐	☐
		☐	☐	☐	☐
		☐	☐	☐	☐
		☐	☐	☐	☐
		☐	☐	☐	☐
Total Income	$				
minus - Total Cash Envelopes	$				
Remaining Balance	$				

Double Check It! Calculations

Cash Breakdown

Date:

CASH ENVELOPES/SINKING FUNDS

CATEGORY	AMOUNT	BANKING WITHDRAWAL DENOMINATIONS					
		$1	$5	$10	$20	$50	$100
		Total Number of Each Bill					
TOTAL	$						

INCOME

INCOME SOURCE	AMOUNT	Salary/Wages	Investment	Business	Side-Hustle
Rollover from previous week		☐	☐	☐	☐
		☐	☐	☐	☐
		☐	☐	☐	☐
		☐	☐	☐	☐
		☐	☐	☐	☐
		☐	☐	☐	☐
		☐	☐	☐	☐
		☐	☐	☐	☐
		☐	☐	☐	☐
Total Income	$				
minus - Total Cash Envelopes	$				
Remaining Balance	$				

Double Check It! Calculations

Cash Breakdown

Date:

CASH ENVELOPES/SINKING FUNDS

CATEGORY	AMOUNT	BANKING WITHDRAWAL DENOMINATIONS					
		$1	$5	$10	$20	$50	$100
		Total Number of Each Bill					
TOTAL	$						

INCOME

INCOME SOURCE	AMOUNT	Salary/Wages	Investment	Business	Side-Hustle
Rollover from previous week		☐	☐	☐	☐
		☐	☐	☐	☐
		☐	☐	☐	☐
		☐	☐	☐	☐
		☐	☐	☐	☐
		☐	☐	☐	☐
		☐	☐	☐	☐
		☐	☐	☐	☐
		☐	☐	☐	☐
Total Income	$				
minus - Total Cash Envelopes	$				
Remaining Balance	$				

Double Check It! Calculations

Cash Breakdown

Date:

CASH ENVELOPES/SINKING FUNDS

CATEGORY	AMOUNT	BANKING WITHDRAWAL DENOMINATIONS					
		$1	$5	$10	$20	$50	$100
		Total Number of Each Bill					
TOTAL	$						

INCOME

INCOME SOURCE	AMOUNT	Salary/Wages	Investment	Business	Side-Hustle
Rollover from previous week		☐	☐	☐	☐
		☐	☐	☐	☐
		☐	☐	☐	☐
		☐	☐	☐	☐
		☐	☐	☐	☐
		☐	☐	☐	☐
		☐	☐	☐	☐
		☐	☐	☐	☐
		☐	☐	☐	☐
Total Income	$				
minus - Total Cash Envelopes	$				
Remaining Balance	$				

Double Check It! Calculations

Cash Breakdown

Date:

CASH ENVELOPES/SINKING FUNDS

CATEGORY	AMOUNT	BANKING WITHDRAWAL DENOMINATIONS					
		$1	$5	$10	$20	$50	$100
		Total Number of Each Bill					
TOTAL	$						

INCOME

INCOME SOURCE	AMOUNT	Salary/Wages	Investment	Business	Side-Hustle
Rollover from previous week		☐	☐	☐	☐
		☐	☐	☐	☐
		☐	☐	☐	☐
		☐	☐	☐	☐
		☐	☐	☐	☐
		☐	☐	☐	☐
		☐	☐	☐	☐
		☐	☐	☐	☐
		☐	☐	☐	☐
Total Income	$				
minus - Total Cash Envelopes	$				
Remaining Balance	$				

Double Check It! Calculations

Cash Breakdown

Date:

CASH ENVELOPES/SINKING FUNDS

CATEGORY	AMOUNT	BANKING WITHDRAWAL DENOMINATIONS					
		$1	$5	$10	$20	$50	$100
		Total Number of Each Bill					
TOTAL	$						

INCOME

INCOME SOURCE	AMOUNT	Salary/Wages	Investment	Business	Side-Hustle
Rollover from previous week		☐	☐	☐	☐
		☐	☐	☐	☐
		☐	☐	☐	☐
		☐	☐	☐	☐
		☐	☐	☐	☐
		☐	☐	☐	☐
		☐	☐	☐	☐
		☐	☐	☐	☐
		☐	☐	☐	☐
Total Income	$				
minus - Total Cash Envelopes	$				
Remaining Balance	$				

Double Check It! Calculations

Cash Breakdown

Date:

CASH ENVELOPES/SINKING FUNDS

CATEGORY	AMOUNT	BANKING WITHDRAWAL DENOMINATIONS					
		$1	$5	$10	$20	$50	$100
		Total Number of Each Bill					
TOTAL	$						

INCOME

INCOME SOURCE	AMOUNT	Salary/Wages	Investment	Business	Side-Hustle
Rollover from previous week		☐	☐	☐	☐
		☐	☐	☐	☐
		☐	☐	☐	☐
		☐	☐	☐	☐
		☐	☐	☐	☐
		☐	☐	☐	☐
		☐	☐	☐	☐
		☐	☐	☐	☐
		☐	☐	☐	☐
Total Income	$				
minus - Total Cash Envelopes	$				
Remaining Balance	$				

Double Check It! Calculations

Cash Breakdown

Date:

CASH ENVELOPES/SINKING FUNDS

CATEGORY	AMOUNT	BANKING WITHDRAWAL DENOMINATIONS					
		$1	$5	$10	$20	$50	$100
		Total Number of Each Bill					
TOTAL	$						

INCOME

INCOME SOURCE	AMOUNT	Salary/Wages	Investment	Business	Side-Hustle
Rollover from previous week		☐	☐	☐	☐
		☐	☐	☐	☐
		☐	☐	☐	☐
		☐	☐	☐	☐
		☐	☐	☐	☐
		☐	☐	☐	☐
		☐	☐	☐	☐
		☐	☐	☐	☐
		☐	☐	☐	☐
Total Income	$				
minus - Total Cash Envelopes	$				
Remaining Balance	$				

Double Check It! Calculations

Cash Breakdown

Date:

CASH ENVELOPES/SINKING FUNDS

CATEGORY	AMOUNT	BANKING WITHDRAWAL DENOMINATIONS					
		$1	$5	$10	$20	$50	$100
		Total Number of Each Bill					
TOTAL	$						

INCOME

INCOME SOURCE	AMOUNT	Salary/Wages	Investment	Business	Side-Hustle
Rollover from previous week		☐	☐	☐	☐
		☐	☐	☐	☐
		☐	☐	☐	☐
		☐	☐	☐	☐
		☐	☐	☐	☐
		☐	☐	☐	☐
		☐	☐	☐	☐
		☐	☐	☐	☐
		☐	☐	☐	☐
Total Income	$				
minus - Total Cash Envelopes	$				
Remaining Balance	$				

Double Check It! Calculations

Cash Breakdown

Date:

CASH ENVELOPES/SINKING FUNDS

CATEGORY	AMOUNT	BANKING WITHDRAWAL DENOMINATIONS					
		$1	$5	$10	$20	$50	$100
		Total Number of Each Bill					
TOTAL	$						

INCOME

INCOME SOURCE	AMOUNT	Salary/Wages	Investment	Business	Side-Hustle
Rollover from previous week		☐	☐	☐	☐
		☐	☐	☐	☐
		☐	☐	☐	☐
		☐	☐	☐	☐
		☐	☐	☐	☐
		☐	☐	☐	☐
		☐	☐	☐	☐
		☐	☐	☐	☐
		☐	☐	☐	☐
Total Income	$				
minus - Total Cash Envelopes	$				
Remaining Balance	$				

Double Check It! Calculations

Cash Breakdown

Date:

CASH ENVELOPES/SINKING FUNDS

CATEGORY	AMOUNT	BANKING WITHDRAWAL DENOMINATIONS					
		$1	$5	$10	$20	$50	$100
		Total Number of Each Bill					
TOTAL	$						

INCOME

INCOME SOURCE	AMOUNT	Salary/Wages	Investment	Business	Side-Hustle
Rollover from previous week		☐	☐	☐	☐
		☐	☐	☐	☐
		☐	☐	☐	☐
		☐	☐	☐	☐
		☐	☐	☐	☐
		☐	☐	☐	☐
		☐	☐	☐	☐
		☐	☐	☐	☐
		☐	☐	☐	☐
Total Income	$				
minus - Total Cash Envelopes	$				
Remaining Balance	$				

Double Check It! Calculations

Cash Breakdown

Date:

CASH ENVELOPES/SINKING FUNDS

CATEGORY	AMOUNT	BANKING WITHDRAWAL DENOMINATIONS					
		$1	$5	$10	$20	$50	$100
		Total Number of Each Bill					
TOTAL	$						

INCOME

INCOME SOURCE	AMOUNT	Salary/Wages	Investment	Business	Side-Hustle
Rollover from previous week		☐	☐	☐	☐
		☐	☐	☐	☐
		☐	☐	☐	☐
		☐	☐	☐	☐
		☐	☐	☐	☐
		☐	☐	☐	☐
		☐	☐	☐	☐
		☐	☐	☐	☐
		☐	☐	☐	☐
Total Income	$				
minus - Total Cash Envelopes	$				
Remaining Balance	$				

Double Check It! Calculations

Cash Breakdown

Date:

CASH ENVELOPES/SINKING FUNDS

CATEGORY	AMOUNT	BANKING WITHDRAWAL DENOMINATIONS					
		$1	$5	$10	$20	$50	$100
		Total Number of Each Bill					
TOTAL	$						

INCOME

INCOME SOURCE	AMOUNT	Salary/Wages	Investment	Business	Side-Hustle
Rollover from previous week		☐	☐	☐	☐
		☐	☐	☐	☐
		☐	☐	☐	☐
		☐	☐	☐	☐
		☐	☐	☐	☐
		☐	☐	☐	☐
		☐	☐	☐	☐
		☐	☐	☐	☐
		☐	☐	☐	☐
Total Income	$				
minus - Total Cash Envelopes	$				
Remaining Balance	$				

Double Check It! Calculations

Cash Breakdown

Date:

CASH ENVELOPES/SINKING FUNDS

CATEGORY	AMOUNT	BANKING WITHDRAWAL DENOMINATIONS					
		$1	$5	$10	$20	$50	$100
		Total Number of Each Bill					
TOTAL	$						

INCOME

INCOME SOURCE	AMOUNT	Salary/Wages	Investment	Business	Side-Hustle
Rollover from previous week		☐	☐	☐	☐
		☐	☐	☐	☐
		☐	☐	☐	☐
		☐	☐	☐	☐
		☐	☐	☐	☐
		☐	☐	☐	☐
		☐	☐	☐	☐
		☐	☐	☐	☐
		☐	☐	☐	☐
Total Income	$				
minus - Total Cash Envelopes	$				
Remaining Balance	$				

Double Check It! Calculations

Cash Breakdown

Date:

CASH ENVELOPES/SINKING FUNDS

CATEGORY	AMOUNT	BANKING WITHDRAWAL DENOMINATIONS					
		$1	$5	$10	$20	$50	$100
		Total Number of Each Bill					
TOTAL	$						

INCOME

INCOME SOURCE	AMOUNT	Salary/Wages	Investment	Business	Side-Hustle
Rollover from previous week		☐	☐	☐	☐
		☐	☐	☐	☐
		☐	☐	☐	☐
		☐	☐	☐	☐
		☐	☐	☐	☐
		☐	☐	☐	☐
		☐	☐	☐	☐
		☐	☐	☐	☐
		☐	☐	☐	☐
Total Income	$				
minus - Total Cash Envelopes	$				
Remaining Balance	$				

Double Check It! Calculations

Cash Breakdown

Date:

CASH ENVELOPES/SINKING FUNDS

CATEGORY	AMOUNT	BANKING WITHDRAWAL DENOMINATIONS					
		$1	$5	$10	$20	$50	$100
		Total Number of Each Bill					
TOTAL	$						

INCOME

INCOME SOURCE	AMOUNT	Salary/Wages	Investment	Business	Side-Hustle
Rollover from previous week		☐	☐	☐	☐
		☐	☐	☐	☐
		☐	☐	☐	☐
		☐	☐	☐	☐
		☐	☐	☐	☐
		☐	☐	☐	☐
		☐	☐	☐	☐
		☐	☐	☐	☐
		☐	☐	☐	☐
Total Income	$				
minus - Total Cash Envelopes	$				
Remaining Balance	$				

Double Check It! Calculations

Cash Breakdown

Date:

CASH ENVELOPES/SINKING FUNDS

CATEGORY	AMOUNT	BANKING WITHDRAWAL DENOMINATIONS					
		$1	$5	$10	$20	$50	$100
		Total Number of Each Bill					
TOTAL	$						

INCOME

INCOME SOURCE	AMOUNT	Salary/Wages	Investment	Business	Side-Hustle
Rollover from previous week		☐	☐	☐	☐
		☐	☐	☐	☐
		☐	☐	☐	☐
		☐	☐	☐	☐
		☐	☐	☐	☐
		☐	☐	☐	☐
		☐	☐	☐	☐
		☐	☐	☐	☐
		☐	☐	☐	☐
Total Income	$				
minus - Total Cash Envelopes	$				
Remaining Balance	$				

Double Check It! Calculations

Cash Breakdown

Date:

CASH ENVELOPES/SINKING FUNDS

CATEGORY	AMOUNT	BANKING WITHDRAWAL DENOMINATIONS					
		$1	$5	$10	$20	$50	$100
		Total Number of Each Bill					
TOTAL	$						

INCOME

INCOME SOURCE	AMOUNT	Salary/Wages	Investment	Business	Side-Hustle
Rollover from previous week		☐	☐	☐	☐
		☐	☐	☐	☐
		☐	☐	☐	☐
		☐	☐	☐	☐
		☐	☐	☐	☐
		☐	☐	☐	☐
		☐	☐	☐	☐
		☐	☐	☐	☐
		☐	☐	☐	☐
Total Income	$				
minus - Total Cash Envelopes	$				
Remaining Balance	$				

Double Check It! Calculations

Cash Breakdown

Date:

CASH ENVELOPES/SINKING FUNDS

CATEGORY	AMOUNT	BANKING WITHDRAWAL DENOMINATIONS					
		$1	$5	$10	$20	$50	$100
		Total Number of Each Bill					
TOTAL	$						

INCOME

INCOME SOURCE	AMOUNT	Salary/Wages	Investment	Business	Side-Hustle
Rollover from previous week		☐	☐	☐	☐
		☐	☐	☐	☐
		☐	☐	☐	☐
		☐	☐	☐	☐
		☐	☐	☐	☐
		☐	☐	☐	☐
		☐	☐	☐	☐
		☐	☐	☐	☐
		☐	☐	☐	☐
Total Income	$				
minus - Total Cash Envelopes	$				
Remaining Balance	$				

Double Check It! Calculations

Cash Breakdown

Date:

CASH ENVELOPES/SINKING FUNDS

CATEGORY	AMOUNT	BANKING WITHDRAWAL DENOMINATIONS					
		$1	$5	$10	$20	$50	$100
		Total Number of Each Bill					
TOTAL	$						

INCOME

INCOME SOURCE	AMOUNT	Salary/Wages	Investment	Business	Side-Hustle
Rollover from previous week		☐	☐	☐	☐
		☐	☐	☐	☐
		☐	☐	☐	☐
		☐	☐	☐	☐
		☐	☐	☐	☐
		☐	☐	☐	☐
		☐	☐	☐	☐
		☐	☐	☐	☐
		☐	☐	☐	☐
Total Income	$				
minus - Total Cash Envelopes	$				
Remaining Balance	$				

Double Check It! Calculations

Cash Breakdown

Date:

CASH ENVELOPES/SINKING FUNDS

CATEGORY	AMOUNT	BANKING WITHDRAWAL DENOMINATIONS					
		$1	$5	$10	$20	$50	$100
		Total Number of Each Bill					
TOTAL	$						

INCOME

INCOME SOURCE	AMOUNT	Salary/Wages	Investment	Business	Side-Hustle
Rollover from previous week		☐	☐	☐	☐
		☐	☐	☐	☐
		☐	☐	☐	☐
		☐	☐	☐	☐
		☐	☐	☐	☐
		☐	☐	☐	☐
		☐	☐	☐	☐
		☐	☐	☐	☐
		☐	☐	☐	☐
Total Income	$				
minus - Total Cash Envelopes	$				
Remaining Balance	$				

Double Check It! Calculations

Cash Breakdown

Date:

CASH ENVELOPES/SINKING FUNDS

CATEGORY	AMOUNT	BANKING WITHDRAWAL DENOMINATIONS					
		$1	$5	$10	$20	$50	$100
		Total Number of Each Bill					
TOTAL	$						

INCOME

INCOME SOURCE	AMOUNT	Salary/Wages	Investment	Business	Side-Hustle
Rollover from previous week		☐	☐	☐	☐
		☐	☐	☐	☐
		☐	☐	☐	☐
		☐	☐	☐	☐
		☐	☐	☐	☐
		☐	☐	☐	☐
		☐	☐	☐	☐
		☐	☐	☐	☐
		☐	☐	☐	☐
Total Income	$				
minus - Total Cash Envelopes	$				
Remaining Balance	$				

Double Check It! Calculations

Cash Breakdown

Date:

CASH ENVELOPES/SINKING FUNDS

CATEGORY	AMOUNT	BANKING WITHDRAWAL DENOMINATIONS					
		$1	$5	$10	$20	$50	$100
		Total Number of Each Bill					
TOTAL	$						

INCOME

INCOME SOURCE	AMOUNT	Salary/Wages	Investment	Business	Side-Hustle
Rollover from previous week		☐	☐	☐	☐
		☐	☐	☐	☐
		☐	☐	☐	☐
		☐	☐	☐	☐
		☐	☐	☐	☐
		☐	☐	☐	☐
		☐	☐	☐	☐
		☐	☐	☐	☐
		☐	☐	☐	☐
Total Income	$				
minus - Total Cash Envelopes	$				
Remaining Balance	$				

Double Check It! Calculations

Cash Breakdown

Date:

CASH ENVELOPES/SINKING FUNDS

CATEGORY	AMOUNT	BANKING WITHDRAWAL DENOMINATIONS					
		$1	$5	$10	$20	$50	$100
		Total Number of Each Bill					
TOTAL	$						

INCOME

INCOME SOURCE	AMOUNT	Salary/Wages	Investment	Business	Side-Hustle
Rollover from previous week		☐	☐	☐	☐
		☐	☐	☐	☐
		☐	☐	☐	☐
		☐	☐	☐	☐
		☐	☐	☐	☐
		☐	☐	☐	☐
		☐	☐	☐	☐
		☐	☐	☐	☐
		☐	☐	☐	☐
Total Income	$				
minus - Total Cash Envelopes	$				
Remaining Balance	$				

Double Check It! Calculations

Cash Breakdown

Date:

CASH ENVELOPES/SINKING FUNDS

CATEGORY	AMOUNT	BANKING WITHDRAWAL DENOMINATIONS					
		$1	$5	$10	$20	$50	$100
		Total Number of Each Bill					
TOTAL	$						

INCOME

INCOME SOURCE	AMOUNT	Salary/Wages	Investment	Business	Side-Hustle
Rollover from previous week		☐	☐	☐	☐
		☐	☐	☐	☐
		☐	☐	☐	☐
		☐	☐	☐	☐
		☐	☐	☐	☐
		☐	☐	☐	☐
		☐	☐	☐	☐
		☐	☐	☐	☐
		☐	☐	☐	☐
Total Income	$				
minus - Total Cash Envelopes	$				
Remaining Balance	$				

Double Check It! Calculations

Cash Breakdown

Date:

CASH ENVELOPES/SINKING FUNDS

CATEGORY	AMOUNT	BANKING WITHDRAWAL DENOMINATIONS					
		$1	$5	$10	$20	$50	$100
		Total Number of Each Bill					
TOTAL	$						

INCOME

INCOME SOURCE	AMOUNT	Salary/Wages	Investment	Business	Side-Hustle
Rollover from previous week		☐	☐	☐	☐
		☐	☐	☐	☐
		☐	☐	☐	☐
		☐	☐	☐	☐
		☐	☐	☐	☐
		☐	☐	☐	☐
		☐	☐	☐	☐
		☐	☐	☐	☐
		☐	☐	☐	☐
Total Income	$				
minus - Total Cash Envelopes	$				
Remaining Balance	$				

Double Check It! Calculations

Cash Breakdown

Date:

CASH ENVELOPES/SINKING FUNDS

CATEGORY	AMOUNT	BANKING WITHDRAWAL DENOMINATIONS					
		$1	$5	$10	$20	$50	$100
		Total Number of Each Bill					
TOTAL	$						

INCOME

INCOME SOURCE	AMOUNT	Salary/Wages	Investment	Business	Side-Hustle
Rollover from previous week		☐	☐	☐	☐
		☐	☐	☐	☐
		☐	☐	☐	☐
		☐	☐	☐	☐
		☐	☐	☐	☐
		☐	☐	☐	☐
		☐	☐	☐	☐
		☐	☐	☐	☐
		☐	☐	☐	☐
Total Income	$				
minus - Total Cash Envelopes	$				
Remaining Balance	$				

Double Check It! Calculations

Cash Breakdown

Date:

CASH ENVELOPES/SINKING FUNDS

CATEGORY	AMOUNT	BANKING WITHDRAWAL DENOMINATIONS					
		$1	$5	$10	$20	$50	$100
		Total Number of Each Bill					
TOTAL	$						

INCOME

INCOME SOURCE	AMOUNT	Salary/Wages	Investment	Business	Side-Hustle
Rollover from previous week		☐	☐	☐	☐
		☐	☐	☐	☐
		☐	☐	☐	☐
		☐	☐	☐	☐
		☐	☐	☐	☐
		☐	☐	☐	☐
		☐	☐	☐	☐
		☐	☐	☐	☐
		☐	☐	☐	☐
Total Income	$				
minus - Total Cash Envelopes	$				
Remaining Balance	$				

Double Check It! Calculations

Cash Breakdown

Date:

CASH ENVELOPES/SINKING FUNDS

CATEGORY	AMOUNT	BANKING WITHDRAWAL DENOMINATIONS					
		$1	$5	$10	$20	$50	$100
		Total Number of Each Bill					
TOTAL	$						

INCOME

INCOME SOURCE	AMOUNT	Salary/Wages	Investment	Business	Side-Hustle
Rollover from previous week		☐	☐	☐	☐
		☐	☐	☐	☐
		☐	☐	☐	☐
		☐	☐	☐	☐
		☐	☐	☐	☐
		☐	☐	☐	☐
		☐	☐	☐	☐
		☐	☐	☐	☐
		☐	☐	☐	☐
Total Income	$				
minus - Total Cash Envelopes	$				
Remaining Balance	$				

Double Check It! Calculations

Cash Breakdown

Date:

CASH ENVELOPES/SINKING FUNDS

CATEGORY	AMOUNT	BANKING WITHDRAWAL DENOMINATIONS					
		$1	$5	$10	$20	$50	$100
		Total Number of Each Bill					
TOTAL	$						

INCOME

INCOME SOURCE	AMOUNT	Salary/Wages	Investment	Business	Side-Hustle
Rollover from previous week		☐	☐	☐	☐
		☐	☐	☐	☐
		☐	☐	☐	☐
		☐	☐	☐	☐
		☐	☐	☐	☐
		☐	☐	☐	☐
		☐	☐	☐	☐
		☐	☐	☐	☐
		☐	☐	☐	☐
Total Income	$				
minus - Total Cash Envelopes	$				
Remaining Balance	$				

Double Check It! Calculations

Cash Breakdown

Date:

CASH ENVELOPES/SINKING FUNDS

CATEGORY	AMOUNT	BANKING WITHDRAWAL DENOMINATIONS					
		$1	$5	$10	$20	$50	$100
		Total Number of Each Bill					
TOTAL	$						

INCOME

INCOME SOURCE	AMOUNT	Salary/Wages	Investment	Business	Side-Hustle
Rollover from previous week		☐	☐	☐	☐
		☐	☐	☐	☐
		☐	☐	☐	☐
		☐	☐	☐	☐
		☐	☐	☐	☐
		☐	☐	☐	☐
		☐	☐	☐	☐
		☐	☐	☐	☐
		☐	☐	☐	☐
Total Income	$				
minus - Total Cash Envelopes	$				
Remaining Balance	$				

Double Check It! Calculations

Cash Breakdown

Date:

CASH ENVELOPES/SINKING FUNDS

CATEGORY	AMOUNT	BANKING WITHDRAWAL DENOMINATIONS					
		$1	$5	$10	$20	$50	$100
		Total Number of Each Bill					
TOTAL	$						

INCOME

INCOME SOURCE	AMOUNT	Salary/Wages	Investment	Business	Side-Hustle
Rollover from previous week		☐	☐	☐	☐
		☐	☐	☐	☐
		☐	☐	☐	☐
		☐	☐	☐	☐
		☐	☐	☐	☐
		☐	☐	☐	☐
		☐	☐	☐	☐
		☐	☐	☐	☐
		☐	☐	☐	☐
Total Income	$				
minus - Total Cash Envelopes	$				
Remaining Balance	$				

Double Check It! Calculations

Cash Breakdown

Date:

CASH ENVELOPES/SINKING FUNDS

CATEGORY	AMOUNT	BANKING WITHDRAWAL DENOMINATIONS					
		$1	$5	$10	$20	$50	$100
		Total Number of Each Bill					
TOTAL	$						

INCOME

INCOME SOURCE	AMOUNT	Salary/Wages	Investment	Business	Side-Hustle
Rollover from previous week		☐	☐	☐	☐
		☐	☐	☐	☐
		☐	☐	☐	☐
		☐	☐	☐	☐
		☐	☐	☐	☐
		☐	☐	☐	☐
		☐	☐	☐	☐
		☐	☐	☐	☐
		☐	☐	☐	☐
Total Income	$				
minus - Total Cash Envelopes	$				
Remaining Balance	$				

Double Check It! Calculations

Cash Breakdown

Date:

CASH ENVELOPES/SINKING FUNDS

CATEGORY	AMOUNT	BANKING WITHDRAWAL DENOMINATIONS					
		$1	$5	$10	$20	$50	$100
		Total Number of Each Bill					
TOTAL	$						

INCOME

INCOME SOURCE	AMOUNT	Salary/Wages	Investment	Business	Side-Hustle
Rollover from previous week		☐	☐	☐	☐
		☐	☐	☐	☐
		☐	☐	☐	☐
		☐	☐	☐	☐
		☐	☐	☐	☐
		☐	☐	☐	☐
		☐	☐	☐	☐
		☐	☐	☐	☐
		☐	☐	☐	☐
Total Income	$				
minus - Total Cash Envelopes	$				
Remaining Balance	$				

Double Check It! Calculations

Cash Breakdown

Date:

CASH ENVELOPES/SINKING FUNDS

CATEGORY	AMOUNT	BANKING WITHDRAWAL DENOMINATIONS					
		$1	$5	$10	$20	$50	$100
		Total Number of Each Bill					
TOTAL	$						

INCOME

INCOME SOURCE	AMOUNT	Salary/Wages	Investment	Business	Side-Hustle
Rollover from previous week		☐	☐	☐	☐
		☐	☐	☐	☐
		☐	☐	☐	☐
		☐	☐	☐	☐
		☐	☐	☐	☐
		☐	☐	☐	☐
		☐	☐	☐	☐
		☐	☐	☐	☐
		☐	☐	☐	☐
Total Income	$				
minus - Total Cash Envelopes	$				
Remaining Balance	$				

Double Check It! Calculations

Cash Breakdown

Date:

CASH ENVELOPES/SINKING FUNDS

CATEGORY	AMOUNT	BANKING WITHDRAWAL DENOMINATIONS					
		$1	$5	$10	$20	$50	$100
		Total Number of Each Bill					
TOTAL	$						

INCOME

INCOME SOURCE	AMOUNT	Salary/Wages	Investment	Business	Side-Hustle
Rollover from previous week		☐	☐	☐	☐
		☐	☐	☐	☐
		☐	☐	☐	☐
		☐	☐	☐	☐
		☐	☐	☐	☐
		☐	☐	☐	☐
		☐	☐	☐	☐
		☐	☐	☐	☐
		☐	☐	☐	☐
Total Income	$				
minus - Total Cash Envelopes	$				
Remaining Balance	$				

Double Check It! Calculations

Cash Breakdown

Date:

CASH ENVELOPES/SINKING FUNDS

CATEGORY	AMOUNT	BANKING WITHDRAWAL DENOMINATIONS					
		$1	$5	$10	$20	$50	$100
		Total Number of Each Bill					
TOTAL	$						

INCOME

INCOME SOURCE	AMOUNT	Salary/Wages	Investment	Business	Side-Hustle
Rollover from previous week		☐	☐	☐	☐
		☐	☐	☐	☐
		☐	☐	☐	☐
		☐	☐	☐	☐
		☐	☐	☐	☐
		☐	☐	☐	☐
		☐	☐	☐	☐
		☐	☐	☐	☐
		☐	☐	☐	☐
Total Income	$				
minus - Total Cash Envelopes	$				
Remaining Balance	$				

Double Check It! Calculations

Cash Breakdown

Date:

CASH ENVELOPES/SINKING FUNDS

CATEGORY	AMOUNT	BANKING WITHDRAWAL DENOMINATIONS					
		$1	$5	$10	$20	$50	$100
		Total Number of Each Bill					
TOTAL	$						

INCOME

INCOME SOURCE	AMOUNT	Salary/Wages	Investment	Business	Side-Hustle
Rollover from previous week		☐	☐	☐	☐
		☐	☐	☐	☐
		☐	☐	☐	☐
		☐	☐	☐	☐
		☐	☐	☐	☐
		☐	☐	☐	☐
		☐	☐	☐	☐
		☐	☐	☐	☐
		☐	☐	☐	☐
Total Income	$				
minus - Total Cash Envelopes	$				
Remaining Balance	$				

Double Check It! Calculations

Cash Breakdown

Date:

CASH ENVELOPES/SINKING FUNDS

CATEGORY	AMOUNT	BANKING WITHDRAWAL DENOMINATIONS					
		$1	$5	$10	$20	$50	$100
		Total Number of Each Bill					
TOTAL	$						

INCOME

INCOME SOURCE	AMOUNT	Salary/Wages	Investment	Business	Side-Hustle
Rollover from previous week		☐	☐	☐	☐
		☐	☐	☐	☐
		☐	☐	☐	☐
		☐	☐	☐	☐
		☐	☐	☐	☐
		☐	☐	☐	☐
		☐	☐	☐	☐
		☐	☐	☐	☐
		☐	☐	☐	☐
Total Income	$				
minus - Total Cash Envelopes	$				
Remaining Balance	$				

Double Check It! Calculations

Cash Breakdown

Date:

CASH ENVELOPES/SINKING FUNDS

CATEGORY	AMOUNT	BANKING WITHDRAWAL DENOMINATIONS					
		$1	$5	$10	$20	$50	$100
		Total Number of Each Bill					
TOTAL	$						

INCOME

INCOME SOURCE	AMOUNT	Salary/Wages	Investment	Business	Side-Hustle
Rollover from previous week		☐	☐	☐	☐
		☐	☐	☐	☐
		☐	☐	☐	☐
		☐	☐	☐	☐
		☐	☐	☐	☐
		☐	☐	☐	☐
		☐	☐	☐	☐
		☐	☐	☐	☐
		☐	☐	☐	☐
Total Income	$				
minus - Total Cash Envelopes	$				
Remaining Balance	$				

Double Check It! Calculations

Cash Breakdown

Date:

CASH ENVELOPES/SINKING FUNDS

CATEGORY	AMOUNT	BANKING WITHDRAWAL DENOMINATIONS					
		$1	$5	$10	$20	$50	$100
		Total Number of Each Bill					
TOTAL	$						

INCOME

INCOME SOURCE	AMOUNT	Salary/Wages	Investment	Business	Side-Hustle
Rollover from previous week		☐	☐	☐	☐
		☐	☐	☐	☐
		☐	☐	☐	☐
		☐	☐	☐	☐
		☐	☐	☐	☐
		☐	☐	☐	☐
		☐	☐	☐	☐
		☐	☐	☐	☐
		☐	☐	☐	☐
Total Income	$				
minus - Total Cash Envelopes	$				
Remaining Balance	$				

Double Check It! Calculations

Cash Breakdown

Date:

CASH ENVELOPES/SINKING FUNDS

CATEGORY	AMOUNT	BANKING WITHDRAWAL DENOMINATIONS					
		$1	$5	$10	$20	$50	$100
		Total Number of Each Bill					
TOTAL	$						

INCOME

INCOME SOURCE	AMOUNT	Salary/Wages	Investment	Business	Side-Hustle
Rollover from previous week		☐	☐	☐	☐
		☐	☐	☐	☐
		☐	☐	☐	☐
		☐	☐	☐	☐
		☐	☐	☐	☐
		☐	☐	☐	☐
		☐	☐	☐	☐
		☐	☐	☐	☐
		☐	☐	☐	☐
Total Income	$				
minus - Total Cash Envelopes	$				
Remaining Balance	$				

Double Check It! Calculations

Cash Breakdown

Date:

CASH ENVELOPES/SINKING FUNDS

CATEGORY	AMOUNT	BANKING WITHDRAWAL DENOMINATIONS					
		$1	$5	$10	$20	$50	$100
		Total Number of Each Bill					
TOTAL	$						

INCOME

INCOME SOURCE	AMOUNT	Salary/Wages	Investment	Business	Side-Hustle
Rollover from previous week		☐	☐	☐	☐
		☐	☐	☐	☐
		☐	☐	☐	☐
		☐	☐	☐	☐
		☐	☐	☐	☐
		☐	☐	☐	☐
		☐	☐	☐	☐
		☐	☐	☐	☐
		☐	☐	☐	☐
Total Income	$				
minus - Total Cash Envelopes	$				
Remaining Balance	$				

Double Check It! Calculations

Cash Breakdown

Date:

CASH ENVELOPES/SINKING FUNDS

CATEGORY	AMOUNT	BANKING WITHDRAWAL DENOMINATIONS					
		$1	$5	$10	$20	$50	$100
		Total Number of Each Bill					
TOTAL	$						

INCOME

INCOME SOURCE	AMOUNT	Salary/Wages	Investment	Business	Side-Hustle
Rollover from previous week		☐	☐	☐	☐
		☐	☐	☐	☐
		☐	☐	☐	☐
		☐	☐	☐	☐
		☐	☐	☐	☐
		☐	☐	☐	☐
		☐	☐	☐	☐
		☐	☐	☐	☐
		☐	☐	☐	☐
Total Income	$				
minus - Total Cash Envelopes	$				
Remaining Balance	$				

Double Check It! Calculations

Cash Breakdown

Date:

CASH ENVELOPES/SINKING FUNDS

CATEGORY	AMOUNT	BANKING WITHDRAWAL DENOMINATIONS					
		$1	$5	$10	$20	$50	$100
		Total Number of Each Bill					
TOTAL	$						

INCOME

INCOME SOURCE	AMOUNT	Salary/Wages	Investment	Business	Side-Hustle
Rollover from previous week		☐	☐	☐	☐
		☐	☐	☐	☐
		☐	☐	☐	☐
		☐	☐	☐	☐
		☐	☐	☐	☐
		☐	☐	☐	☐
		☐	☐	☐	☐
		☐	☐	☐	☐
		☐	☐	☐	☐
Total Income	$				
minus - Total Cash Envelopes	$				
Remaining Balance	$				

Double Check It! Calculations

Cash Breakdown

Date:

CASH ENVELOPES/SINKING FUNDS

CATEGORY	AMOUNT	BANKING WITHDRAWAL DENOMINATIONS					
		$1	$5	$10	$20	$50	$100
		Total Number of Each Bill					
TOTAL	$						

INCOME

INCOME SOURCE	AMOUNT	Salary/Wages	Investment	Business	Side-Hustle
Rollover from previous week		☐	☐	☐	☐
		☐	☐	☐	☐
		☐	☐	☐	☐
		☐	☐	☐	☐
		☐	☐	☐	☐
		☐	☐	☐	☐
		☐	☐	☐	☐
		☐	☐	☐	☐
		☐	☐	☐	☐
Total Income	$				
minus - Total Cash Envelopes	$				
Remaining Balance	$				

Double Check It! Calculations

Cash Breakdown

Date:

CASH ENVELOPES/SINKING FUNDS

CATEGORY	AMOUNT	BANKING WITHDRAWAL DENOMINATIONS					
		$1	$5	$10	$20	$50	$100
		Total Number of Each Bill					
TOTAL	$						

INCOME

INCOME SOURCE	AMOUNT	Salary/Wages	Investment	Business	Sice-Hustle
Rollover from previous week		☐	☐	☐	☐
		☐	☐	☐	☐
		☐	☐	☐	☐
		☐	☐	☐	☐
		☐	☐	☐	☐
		☐	☐	☐	☐
		☐	☐	☐	☐
		☐	☐	☐	☐
		☐	☐	☐	☐
Total Income	$				
minus - Total Cash Envelopes	$				
Remaining Balance	$				

Double Check It! Calculations

Cash Breakdown

Date:

CASH ENVELOPES/SINKING FUNDS

CATEGORY	AMOUNT	BANKING WITHDRAWAL DENOMINATIONS					
		$1	$5	$10	$20	$50	$100
		Total Number of Each Bill					
TOTAL	$						

INCOME

INCOME SOURCE	AMOUNT	Salary/Wages	Investment	Business	Side-Hustle
Rollover from previous week		☐	☐	☐	☐
		☐	☐	☐	☐
		☐	☐	☐	☐
		☐	☐	☐	☐
		☐	☐	☐	☐
		☐	☐	☐	☐
		☐	☐	☐	☐
		☐	☐	☐	☐
		☐	☐	☐	☐
Total Income	$				
minus - Total Cash Envelopes	$				
Remaining Balance	$				

Double Check It! Calculations

Cash Breakdown

Date:

CASH ENVELOPES/SINKING FUNDS

CATEGORY	AMOUNT	BANKING WITHDRAWAL DENOMINATIONS					
		$1	$5	$10	$20	$50	$100
		Total Number of Each Bill					
TOTAL	$						

INCOME

INCOME SOURCE	AMOUNT	Salary/Wages	Investment	Business	Side-Hustle
Rollover from previous week		☐	☐	☐	☐
		☐	☐	☐	☐
		☐	☐	☐	☐
		☐	☐	☐	☐
		☐	☐	☐	☐
		☐	☐	☐	☐
		☐	☐	☐	☐
		☐	☐	☐	☐
		☐	☐	☐	☐
Total Income	$				
minus - Total Cash Envelopes	$				
Remaining Balance	$				

Double Check It! Calculations

Cash Breakdown

Date:

CASH ENVELOPES/SINKING FUNDS

CATEGORY	AMOUNT	BANKING WITHDRAWAL DENOMINATIONS					
		$1	$5	$10	$20	$50	$100
		Total Number of Each Bill					
TOTAL	$						

INCOME

INCOME SOURCE	AMOUNT	Salary/Wages	Investment	Business	Side-Hustle
Rollover from previous week		☐	☐	☐	☐
		☐	☐	☐	☐
		☐	☐	☐	☐
		☐	☐	☐	☐
		☐	☐	☐	☐
		☐	☐	☐	☐
		☐	☐	☐	☐
		☐	☐	☐	☐
		☐	☐	☐	☐
Total Income	$				
minus - Total Cash Envelopes	$				
Remaining Balance	$				

Double Check It! Calculations

Cash Breakdown

Date:

CASH ENVELOPES/SINKING FUNDS

CATEGORY	AMOUNT	BANKING WITHDRAWAL DENOMINATIONS					
		$1	$5	$10	$20	$50	$100
		Total Number of Each Bill					
TOTAL	$						

INCOME

INCOME SOURCE	AMOUNT	Salary/Wages	Investment	Business	Side-Hustle
Rollover from previous week		☐	☐	☐	☐
		☐	☐	☐	☐
		☐	☐	☐	☐
		☐	☐	☐	☐
		☐	☐	☐	☐
		☐	☐	☐	☐
		☐	☐	☐	☐
		☐	☐	☐	☐
		☐	☐	☐	☐
Total Income	$				
minus - Total Cash Envelopes	$				
Remaining Balance	$				

Double Check It! Calculations

Cash Breakdown

Date:

CASH ENVELOPES/SINKING FUNDS

CATEGORY	AMOUNT	BANKING WITHDRAWAL DENOMINATIONS					
		$1	$5	$10	$20	$50	$100
		Total Number of Each Bill					
TOTAL	$						

INCOME

INCOME SOURCE	AMOUNT	Salary/Wages	Investment	Business	Side-Hustle
Rollover from previous week		☐	☐	☐	☐
		☐	☐	☐	☐
		☐	☐	☐	☐
		☐	☐	☐	☐
		☐	☐	☐	☐
		☐	☐	☐	☐
		☐	☐	☐	☐
		☐	☐	☐	☐
		☐	☐	☐	☐
Total Income	$				
minus - Total Cash Envelopes	$				
Remaining Balance	$				

Double Check It! Calculations

Made in the USA
Monee, IL
04 November 2026

67374637R00038

A Shonversation Book
Budget/Personal Finance

U.S. $18.00
CAN. $20.00

ISBN 9781949210057
90000
9 781949 210057

DOGGY & ME

LUXDIOR.CO

Vol 2.

MASTER THE ART OF GOURMET PET CUISINE:
ELEVATE YOUR PUP'S DINING EXPERIENCE WITH EXPERT RECIPES

38 GOURMET
RECIPES FOR YOU & YOUR PUP

RAISE A PAW TO DOGGY HAPPY HOUR:
INDULGE YOUR PUP WITH LUX DIOR DOGGY BEER, BOW WOW BOURBON, DOG TEAQUILA...
THE ULTIMATE CANINE COCKTAILS!

Follow us on
LUXDIOR.CO

LUXDIOR.CO
By Dee DeVaughn